RED FOX

Jinny Johnson

Illustrations by Graham Rosewarne

FRANKLIN WATTS
LONDON•SYDNEY

 An Appleseed Editions book

First published in 2009 by Franklin Watts
338 Euston Road, London NW1 3BH

Franklin Watts Australia
Hachette Children's Books
Level 17/207 Kent St, Sydney, NSW 2000

© 2009 Appleseed Editions

Created by Appleseed Editions Ltd,
Well House, Friars Hill, Guestling,
East Sussex TN35 4ET

Designed by Helen James
Edited by Mary-Jane Wilkins
Picture research by Su Alexander

ISBN 978 0 7496 8785 4

Dewey Classification: 599.775

A CIP catalogue for this book is available from the British Library.

Photograph acknowledgements
page 9 Phyllis Greenberg/Photolibrary Group;
13 AlaskaStock/Photolibrary Group; 23 Photolibrary Group;
29 Elliott Neep/Photolibrary Group
Front cover Elliott Neep/Photolibrary Group

Printed in China

Franklin Watts is a division of Hachette Children's Books,
an Hachette Livre UK company.
www.hachettelivre.co.ukwww.hachettelivre.co.uk

Contents

First days

These **baby foxes** were born just a few days ago. They lie **snuggled up** to their mother in their den. The den is a **hole dug in the ground**. It may be near a hedge or by a tree or even under a garden shed.

A **baby fox is tiny** and he cannot see or hear. He's not much longer than your hand and **he weighs less than an apple**. His soft dark fur keeps him warm.

Baby foxes are called **cubs or kits**. All they can do at the moment is sleep and eat.

MUM KEEPS THE BABY FOXES SAFE AND WARM.

The baby fox is hungry. What does he eat?

Inside the den

Mum's milk is all the cubs need for the first few weeks of their lives. Her milk is **rich** and the cubs **grow fast**.

The mother fox doesn't leave her family. Her **mate brings food to her** in the den so she doesn't need to go hunting.

When a fox cub is about two weeks old his **eyes begin to open**. He starts to **explore the den** with his brothers and sisters. But they are not big enough to go outside yet.

THE MALE FOX BRINGS FOOD TO HIS MATE, BUT THE CUBS FEED ON MILK FROM THEIR MOTHER.

The baby fox is growing bigger.
When will he go outside?

What's outside?

When he is about four weeks old the **fox cub** peeks out of the den for the first time. He and his brothers and sisters don't dare go far from home.

If they **get scared** they call to their mum and she comes **running to the rescue**. Mum gently **picks up the cubs** by the skin at the back of the neck and carries them back to the den.

Soon the cub's **baby fur** begins to fall out and he grows **a new reddish coat**. He begins to look more like his mum and dad.

THE WORLD OUTSIDE THE
DEN LOOKS SCARY AT FIRST.

*What do the fox cubs
do when they go outside?*

Playtime

The cubs have **lots of fun** when they're outside. They are **very curious about the world** and they **sniff** and **chew** anything they find.

Chase is the cubs' favourite game and they like to **sneak up and pounce** on each other. They love to play, but they are also practising for when they are **fully grown**. Then they will **hunt and catch** other animals to eat.

What do the cubs eat now?

What's for supper?

The growing cubs are very hungry and **need more food** now. Their mother and father bring them other kinds of food, such as **mice and voles**.

When mum and dad arrive with a meal they **call to the cubs**. The cubs rush up as fast as they can, **yelping** and **wagging** their tails. They can't wait for their food and may **fight over it**.

The parents start to leave food further away from the den to encourage the **cubs to explore**.

THE CUBS CAN'T
CATCH THEIR OWN
FOOD YET.

When will the cubs start to learn to hunt?

Lots to learn

At three months the cubs are **big** enough to follow their parents when they go **hunting for food**. At first the cubs watch and learn. They have to find out what is good to eat.

When the family is out and about mum keeps a close eye on the cubs. If she's worried she has a **special bark**. The cubs know this means **danger**.

The cubs look more like their parents now. Their ears are bigger and their **faces are longer** and narrower.

What do the cubs try to catch?

Hunting practice

The first creatures the cubs learn to catch are **worms and beetles**. They listen carefully to hear them moving along the ground and then **pounce**.

Foxes eat **mice, rabbits, squirrels** and other creatures too, but the cubs need more practice at catching these.

Like their parents, the cubs gobble up **lots of berries** and other fruits during the summer. They pick up food left or **thrown away by humans** too.

Catching small creatures such as
worms is good hunting practice.

When will the cubs be full grown?

Time to leave

At six months the cubs are almost **as big as their mum** and weigh a bit more than a pet cat. They will soon be able to **live on their own**.

The parents bring less food now. The cubs have to **hunt for themselves** most of the time and it's not always easy.

The cubs can **run fast** to escape from danger. They also **chase fast prey animals**. They have lots of sharp teeth for eating their **catch**.

YOUNG FOXES MUST LEARN HOW TO WATCH AND CREEP UP ON PREY.

Are the cubs ready to leave home?

Finding a home

In **autumn** the cubs **leave**.
There is not enough food for
them all nearby, so the young
foxes go **somewhere else to live**.

If a young male wanders into
an area where another fox is
living he will be **attacked** and
driven away. When he finds a safe
place he **marks the trees**, fences
or walls with **his own scent** so
other animals know that he is there.

A female cub may stay with
her parents longer. **If there is
lots of food** she may help mum
raise her cubs **next spring**.

A FOX MARKS
ITS HOME
RANGE WITH
ITS WEE.

What does the young fox do all by himself?

Living alone

When **the young fox** has found
a place to live he spends a lot of time
finding food. He's always on the
lookout for a meal.

His hearing is so good that he can
hear **a mouse** scurrying through
the grass so he is ready to pounce.
His **sense of smell** is very keen too.

When the fox finds **lots of food**
he may hide some to eat another time.
He buries it or **covers it with leaves**
and hopes another fox won't find it!

What do foxes do in the winter?

Starting a family

Life is **harder** in **midwinter**. The weather is **cold** and food is hard to find.

Luckily the fox has **thick fur to keep him warm**. When he settles down to sleep he wraps his big **bushy tail** around himself like a **cosy scarf**.

Since leaving his family the fox has been **alone**. But early in the new year he notices a **young vixen** nearby. It is time to start **their own family**.

How do the foxes get ready for their cubs?

New life

The foxes search for a den. It must be big enough for the vixen and her cubs to live in for the **first few weeks**. The den needs to be near **fresh water** but well hidden so they are safe.

After **about seven weeks** the vixen gives birth **in the den** and soon her **tiny cubs** are feeding on her milk.

The **baby foxes** are small now, but this time next year they may be having **cubs of their own**.

THE FOXES NEED A SAFE DEN WHERE THEY CAN BRING UP THEIR FAMILY.

More about foxes

What is a fox?

A fox is a mammal. It belongs to the dog family and is related to dogs, wolves and coyotes. This book is about a red fox but there are other kinds of foxes. Some of the best known are the Arctic fox, which lives in the far north, and the tiny fennec fox found in desert areas of North Africa.

Where does the red fox live?

The red fox is one of the most widespread of all mammals. It lives all over Europe, North Africa, North America and much of Asia. Red foxes were taken to Australia in the 19th century and are now common there. Foxes are very adaptable creatures and can live in woodland or farmland. More and more foxes are taking to life in cities, where they can find plenty of food.

How big is a fox?

A red fox weighs between 4 and 8 kg. Its head and body are 62 to 72 cm long. The bushy tail can be up to 44 cm long. Female foxes are slightly smaller than males.

THE RED FOX IS A CLEVER ANIMAL AND A FAST-MOVING HUNTER.

Words to remember

cub

A young animal.

den

A fox's home, often a hole dug in the ground.

hunting

Finding and catching other animals to eat.

mammal

A warm-blooded animal, usually with four legs and some hair on its body. Female mammals feed their babies with milk from their own bodies.

marks

An animal marks an object such as a tree to put its own smell on it. It's a way of saying, "I live here".

mate

Male and female animals pair up, or mate, to produce young. An animal's partner is called its mate.

prey

An animal that is hunted and eaten by another animal.

scent

Another word for smell.

vixen

A female fox.

vole

A small mammal that looks rather like a mouse.

Websites

BBC Science and Nature
http://www.bbc.co.uk/nature/wildfacts/factfiles/137.shtml

National Geographic
http://animals.nationalgeographic.com/animals/mammals/red-foxhtml

Natureworks
http://www.nhptv.org/NatureWorks/redfox.htm

Index